Ron Rabbit has an egg.
"A chicken will hatch out of this egg," he says.

1

"Then, when that chicken is a hen, it will give me lots of eggs.

If I sell the eggs, I can get a
big pot.

Then I can make lots of jam.

If I sell the jam, I can get a fishing rod.

6

I will catch lots of fish and
sell them.

Then I will be rich! I can have
lots of things.

I can have a hammock and
a big box of chocs.

I can have a chess set.

I can have a tennis racket.

I can play jazz on a sax.

I can have a jacket with lots of pockets and zips and buttons,

and thick mittens, and a hat
with a pompom.

I will be in the jet set!"

But then ... bang!

"That egg had such a thin shell!"
says Ron Rabbit.